W9-CNA-368

Coaches

by Robin Nelson

Lerner Publications Company • Minneapolis

Lerner Publications Company
A division of Lerner Publishing Group
241 First Avenue North
Minneapolis, MN 55401 USA

Website address: www.lernerbooks.com

Words in **bold type** are explained in a glossary on page 31.

Library of Congress Cataloging-in-Publication Data

Nelson, Robin, 1971–
    Coaches / by Robin Nelson.
      p. cm. – (Pull ahead books)
    Includes index.
    ISBN: 0–8225–1686–1 (lib. bdg. : alk. paper)
    1. Coaches (Athletics)–Juvenile literature. I. Title.
  II. Series.
  GV711.N45 2005
  796'.07'7–dc22   2004019563

Manufactured in the United States of America
1 2 3 4 5 6 – JR – 10 09 08 07 06 05

Soccer players are practicing.
Who is blowing the whistle?

A coach is blowing the whistle. Coaches are people who teach sports.

Coaches are a big part of sports in your **community.** Your community is made up of people in your neighborhood, town, or city.

Coaches help decide when to practice. They decide where to have games and which players to play.

Most sports have coaches. Swimming
teams have coaches.

Football teams have coaches.

There are even coaches for dance, such as ballet.

Coaches teach kids and adults. There are coaches for Little League Baseball.

There are coaches for Major League Baseball. That's because players of all ages can get better.

Coaches watch players during games and practices. Coaches tell players how to get better.

Coaches know that the more you practice, the better you can play!

Coaches teach players how to get ready to play. Warming up helps keep you from getting hurt.

Coaches lead players in **drills.**
Players learn moves by doing drills
over and over again.

Coaches bring **equipment** for practices and games.

They show players how to use
the equipment.

Go team! Some coaches do a **cheer** with their team to get them excited before a game.

Every player is important. Coaches
make sure each player gets to play.

Coaches teach players to work together as a team. Coaches like teams that work hard and have fun!

Coaches call **time-outs** to give teams a rest.

Coaches help players know what to do
during a game. Coaches want players
to listen and follow directions.

Coaches teach players the rules of games. Coaches and **referees** make sure games are played the right way.

Coaches also make sure players stay
safe. Coaches take care of hurt players.

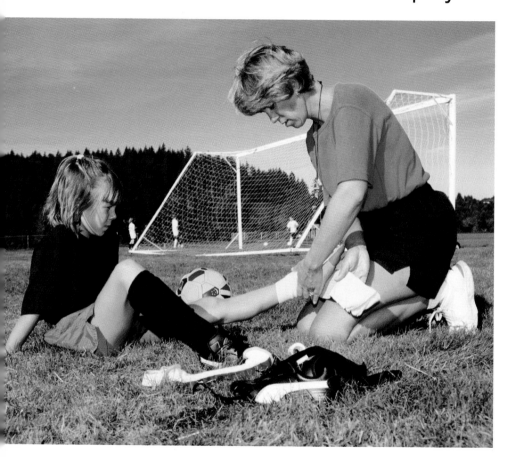

Coaches celebrate when their teams play well. Coaches are proud of their teams even when they lose.

Coaches teach their teams how to be
good sports. Good sports don't brag
when they win. Good sports don't act
upset when they lose.

Coaches are their teams' biggest fans.

Facts about Coaches

■ Coaches have many names. In some sports, coaches are called managers or trainers.

■ Good coaches care about kids and sports. They want their players to have fun. They like sharing what they know about sports.

■ Most coaches used to play the sport they coach. They like the sport so much that they want to help others enjoy it.

■ Both men and women can be coaches.

■ Many football teams have lots of coaches. The head coach has assistant coaches to help him do his job.

■ Some coaches use whistles and stopwatches during practices and games. They also have first-aid kits and phones in case a player gets hurt.

■ Some coaches get paid, but many coaches work with players for free.

Coaches through History

■ Coaches have been around for a long time. Athletes in the first Olympic Games had coaches.

■ Lenny Wilkens was a coach for a team in the National Basketball Association (NBA). He holds the record for the most games won—1,315!

■ Many coaches carry whistles around their necks. The first whistle for sports was invented in 1884. It was called the Acme Thunderer. The Acme Thunderer is the world's best-selling whistle and is still used in many countries.

■ Most coaches don't have uniforms. But many still dress up for games.

More about Coaches

Check out these books and websites to find out more about coaches.

Books

Bowman-Kruhm, Mary, and Claudine G. Wirths. *A Day in the Life of a Coach.* New York: PowerKids Press, 1997.

Flanagan, Alice K. *Coach John and His Soccer Team.* New York: Children's Press, 1998.

Nagle, Jeanne M. *Careers in Coaching.* New York: Rosen Publishing Group, 2000.

Reeves, Diane Lindsey. *Career Ideas for Kids Who Like Sports.* New York: Facts on File, 1998.

Websites

Kids in Sports
http://www.kidsinsports.com/

Sports Illustrated for Kids
http://www.sikids.com/

Glossary

cheer: a shout to fire up a team or player before a game

community: a group of people who live in the same city, town, or neighborhood. Communities share the same fire departments, schools, libraries, and other helpful places.

drills: movements done over and over again to teach players new skills

equipment: gear used in sports, such as baseball bats, basketballs, and ice skates

good sports: players that play fair and are polite whether they win or lose

referees: people who oversee a sports game and make sure that players follow the rules

time-outs: breaks or pauses in sports games so players can rest and get directions from a coach

Index

cheer, 18

community, 5

drills, 15

equipment, 16, 17

games, 6, 12, 16, 18, 22, 23, 28, 29

good sports, 26

hurt, 14, 24, 28

practice, 6, 12, 13, 16, 28

rules, 23

warming up, 14

whistles, 3, 4, 28, 29

Photo Acknowledgments

The photographs in this book appear courtesy of: © BananaStock/SuperStock, front cover, pp. 7, 13, 15, 27; © Myrleen Cate/Photo Network, p. 3; © Bernard Bisson/CORBIS SYGMA, p. 4; © Jim Baron/The Image Fingers, p. 5; © Patti McConville/Photo Network, p. 6; © Joseph D. Poellot/ Index Stock Imagery, p. 8; © Robert Essel NYC/CORBIS, p. 9; © Jim Cummins/CORBIS, p. 10; © SportsChrome East/West/Michael Zito, p. 11; © Jon Feingersh/CORBIS, p. 12; © Mark E. Gibson/The Image Finders, p. 14; © Beth Johnson/Independent Picture Service, pp. 16, 17; © John Welzenbach/CORBIS, p. 18; © Tom Stewart/CORBIS, p. 19; © Mary Messenger/ Photo Network, p. 20; © F. Armstrong/Photo Network, pp. 21, 26; © Huemoeller/Photo Network, p. 22; © Duomo/CORBIS, p. 23; PhotoDisc Royalty Free by Getty Images, p. 24; © LWA-Dann Tardif/CORBIS, p. 25; Library of Congress (LC-USZ62-86972), p. 29.